Langur monkey

These monkeys are [...]
leaf monkeys, bec[...]
eat mainly leaves. [...]
eat fruit, buds, an[...]

D0861746

Tiger

Tigers are the largest
members of the cat
family. They are
fearsome hunters with
sharp teeth, strong
jaws, and powerful
front paws. Tigers
stalk their prey by
hiding in the long grass
until they are close
enough to pounce.
Their orange, black,
and white stripes make
them hard to spot in
the dappled shadows.

Spider monkey

Spider monkeys live high in the jungle treetops. They have long arms and legs, perfect for swinging from branch to branch. They can even grab branches with their long tails.

Gorilla

These large apes live in the rain forests of Africa in small family groups. One adult male takes charge of each group. An adult male gorilla is called a silverback, as it has a patch of silvery hair on its back.

Jungle trail

The tangled treetops of the world's rain forests form a shelter from sun and rain, and also provide homes and food for many different kinds of animals.

Every evening, chimpanzees and gorillas build nests from branches and leaves, which they sleep in for the night.

Babirusa

This Indonesian pig has long, curved tusks. It wallows in muddy hollows, then rubs itself against trees to remove the dried mud and tiny insects that live on its skin.

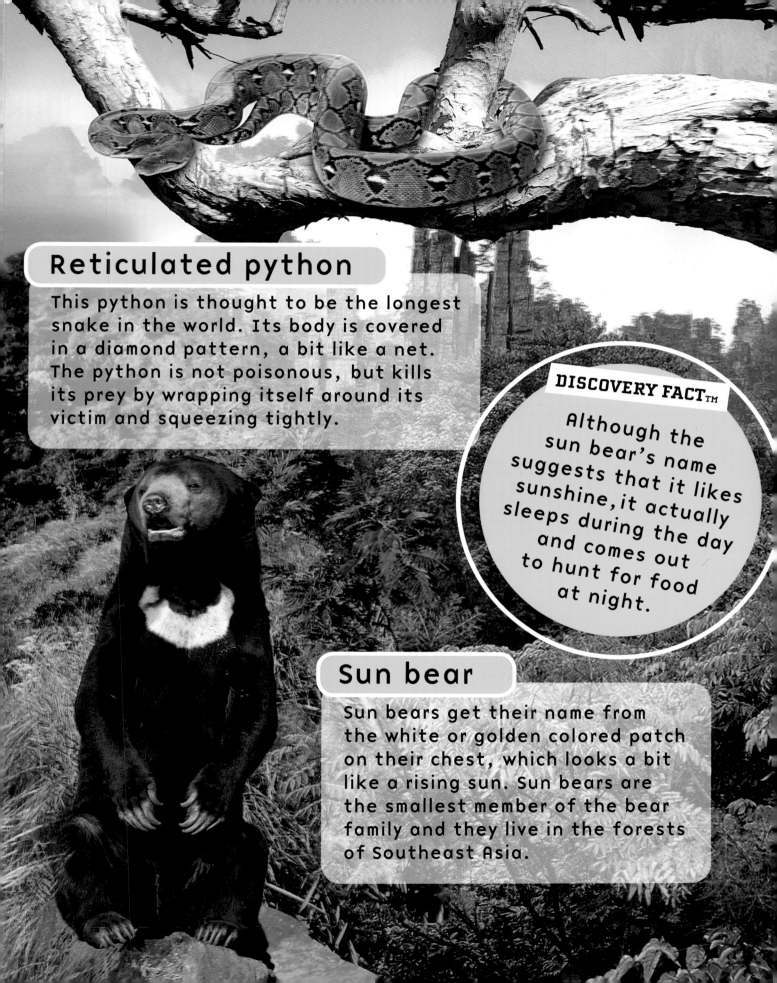

Reticulated python

This python is thought to be the longest snake in the world. Its body is covered in a diamond pattern, a bit like a net. The python is not poisonous, but kills its prey by wrapping itself around its victim and squeezing tightly.

DISCOVERY FACT™

Although the sun bear's name suggests that it likes sunshine, it actually sleeps during the day and comes out to hunt for food at night.

Sun bear

Sun bears get their name from the white or golden colored patch on their chest, which looks a bit like a rising sun. Sun bears are the smallest member of the bear family and they live in the forests of Southeast Asia.

King angelfish

These colorful fish have very flat, upright bodies that allow them to glide effortlessly through the water and turn quickly.

Balloon fish

When a balloon fish is threatened, it takes extra water into its body to inflate itself. Its body is covered in long, sharp spines that stick out when the fish is inflated and warn predators to keep away.

Squirrel monkey

Squirrel monkeys can leap long distances between trees, carrying their babies on their backs.

Ocelot

These graceful cats are about twice the size of a pet cat. They are good swimmers and mainly hunt at night.

Jaguar

Jaguars have incredibly powerful jaws and can bite right through the hard shell of a turtle. They often bury their prey after killing it, so that they can return to eat it later.

Two-toed sloth

Two-toed sloths spend up to 20 hours of every day asleep. They hang upside down in trees, clinging tightly to branches with their long claws.

Howler monkey

These are the loudest of all monkeys. In the morning and evening, they call to let other monkeys know where their territory is, alerting them to stay away. The calls sound like a loud, whooping bark or roar.

Tropical reef

The warm, clear, shallow waters of coral reefs are teeming with life.

A coral reef is made by millions of tiny creatures, called polyps. They build a hard case around their soft bodies.

Clown fish

Clever little clown fish keep their enemies away by swimming among the poisonous tentacles of anemones. The poison kills most fish that touch the tentacles, but clownfish have a special slime covering their scales that protects them from the anemones' deadly sting.

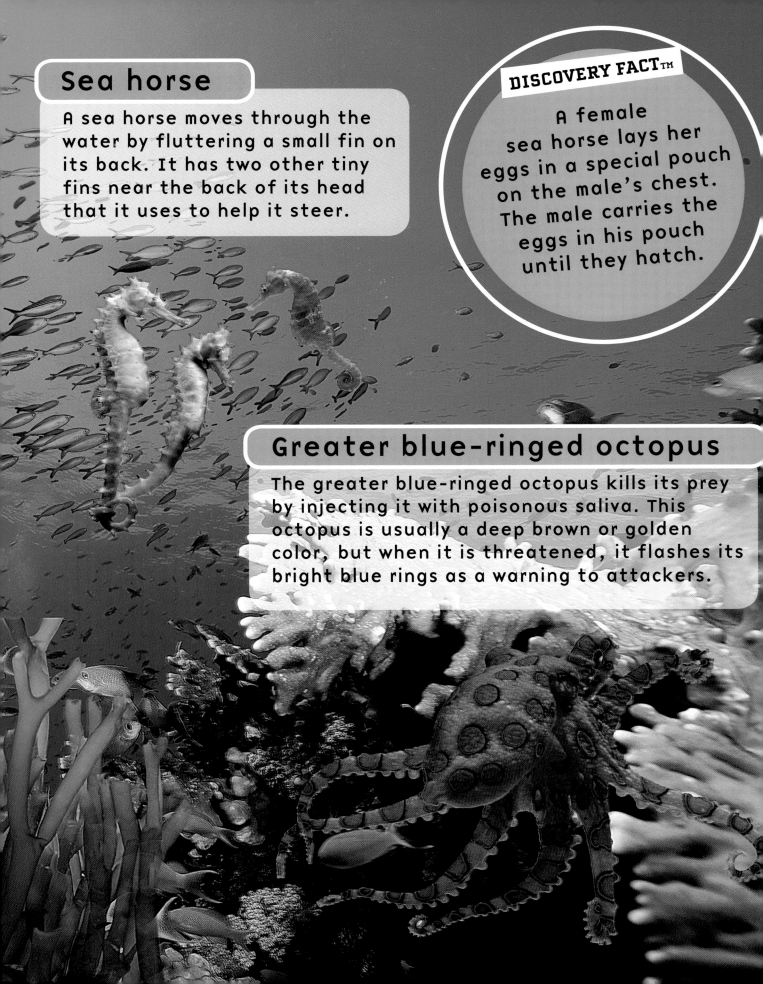

Sea horse

A sea horse moves through the water by fluttering a small fin on its back. It has two other tiny fins near the back of its head that it uses to help it steer.

A female sea horse lays her eggs in a special pouch on the male's chest. The male carries the eggs in his pouch until they hatch.

Greater blue-ringed octopus

The greater blue-ringed octopus kills its prey by injecting it with poisonous saliva. This octopus is usually a deep brown or golden color, but when it is threatened, it flashes its bright blue rings as a warning to attackers.

African safari

Savannahs are flat and windy areas, with scattered trees, grasses, and small bushes. The African savannah is the largest natural grassland in the world and home to many of Africa's biggest and most amazing mammals.

DISCOVERY FACT™

Elephants use their trunk for breathing, smelling, drinking, eating, and bathing, as well as for breaking, and lifting branches.

African elephant

African elephants are the largest living land mammals. They can grow to 10 feet (3 meters) tall. They use their tusks for digging up roots and stripping bark off trees to eat.

Zebra

Every zebra has a totally different striped pattern on its body that is as individual as a human's fingerprint. The stripes help the zebra to hide from predators in the long grass.

Antelope

Antelopes are herbivores (plant-eaters). They have large eyes and ears and they use their keen senses of smell, hearing, and sight to detect predators.

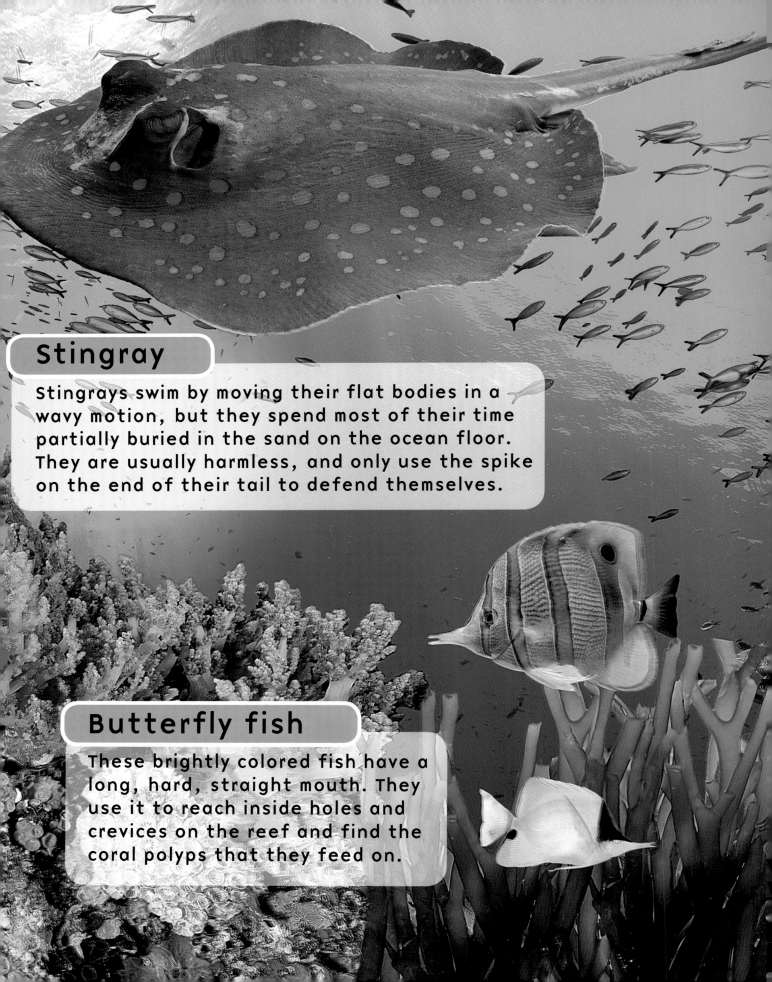

Stingray

Stingrays swim by moving their flat bodies in a wavy motion, but they spend most of their time partially buried in the sand on the ocean floor. They are usually harmless, and only use the spike on the end of their tail to defend themselves.

Butterfly fish

These brightly colored fish have a long, hard, straight mouth. They use it to reach inside holes and crevices on the reef and find the coral polyps that they feed on.

Caiman

Caimans are part of the crocodile family. When they glide underwater, with just their eyes poking out, they look just like floating logs. They use this clever way of disguising themselves to surprise and capture their prey.

Green iguana

Green iguanas are a type of lizard. They move quickly and easily on land. Their powerful legs help them to climb trees or swim away from attackers.

Giraffe

The giraffe is the world's tallest mammal. Its long neck helps it to reach up to the leaves on the tall trees, and reach down to drink. It has a tough, purple-blue tongue that is covered in bristles to help it chew thorny acacia leaves.

African lion

Lions are the only big cats to live in family groups, called prides. The female lions are lighter and faster than the males and they are the main hunters. Lions have an excellent sense of smell for tracking down prey.

White rhinoceros

When the African sun is at its hottest, white rhinos take cover by lying in the shade or wallowing in muddy water holes. The mud works like a sunscreen, protecting the rhino from the sun's harmful rays.

DISCOVERY FACT™
Although a giraffe's neck can grow up to 6 feet (1.8 meters) long, it contains the same number of bones as your neck.

Meerkat

Meerkats search for food in groups. The meerkats take turns to stand guard, watching for danger, while the others find lizards, snakes, scorpions, and spiders to eat.

Amazon odyssey

The giant Amazon River flows through the tropical jungles of South America. Its waters and banks are home to a huge number of animals, including snakes, lizards, and frogs.

Red-eyed tree frog

These tree-dwelling frogs flash their vivid red eyes and show their bright orange feet to predators to try to scare them away.

Some tree frogs have a special sac in their throat, which they can inflate to croak loudly to their mate.

Coral snake

This poisonous snake is a very good swimmer and spends most of its life gliding near riverbanks searching for food. It eats lizards, frogs, and small mammals. As it bites its prey, it injects it with a deadly venom.

Poison dart frog

These eye-catching frogs come in many colors. The bright patterns on their skin warn predators that they are poisonous to eat.

Winged wonders

Meet some colorful tropical butterflies and exotic birds from around the world.

Swallowtail butterfly

There are over 500 different kinds of swallowtails, the largest of which is the giant African swallowtail. Its wings measure up to 9 inches (22 centimeters) from tip to tip.

DISCOVERY FACT™

The smallest bird in the world is the bee hummingbird, which is about the size of a bee!

Hummingbird

These tiny birds hover by beating their wings up to 75 times each second. Their vibrating wings make a humming noise.

Lorikeet

This bright little parrot has an unusual tongue; it is long and narrow, and the end is bristly, like a brush. The bristles help it to lap up the sweet nectar, which is its favorite food.

Monarch butterfly

These butterflies have an easily recognizable orange and black pattern on their wings. The males release special chemicals, called pheromones, which attract female monarchs.

Anaconda

Anacondas are huge snakes that swim in the slow-moving waters of the Amazon River. Like all snakes, they swallow their prey whole, head first. Strong acids in the snakes' stomach digest the food.

DISCOVERY FACT™

The anaconda has a special jaw that can stretch very wide. It swallows animals much bigger than itself, such as deer, pigs, and caimans.

Twilight world

It is hard for most plants and animals to survive in hot, dry deserts such as the Sahara. Some animals have developed special ways of coping with the long, dry periods. Many desert creatures keep out of the sun during the hottest parts of the day and look for food at night when it's cooler.

African pygmy hedgehog

These spiky little animals survive the hot desert summers by sleeping through them. They scuttle out at night to find tasty insects to eat.

Laughing kookaburra

As its name suggests, the laughing kookaburra has a call that sounds like laughter. It lives in the eucalyptus forests of eastern Australia and eats large insects, lizards, small birds, and sometimes snakes.

DISCOVERY FACT™

A toucan's long beak allows it to reach deep inside tree-holes to find food that other birds cannot reach.

Toucan

Toucans aren't very good at flying and they spend most of their time hopping between the rain forest trees. They have brightly colored bills (or beaks) which they use to cut down fruit from the trees.

Cockatoo

Cockatoos come in many different colors, but usually have an impressive crest of feathers on the top of their head, and a short, curved beak.

Bird of paradise

These beautiful birds have stunning feathers of yellow, green, red, and blue. The male birds show off their feathers to the females, and often dance and pose for hours to attract their attention.

There is very little water to drink in the desert. Many animals survive on the liquid they get from the food that they eat.

Hyena

Hyenas hunt in packs, working together to chase after prey. They mainly hunt for food at night, using the darkness to get closer to their prey without being seen.